EAT DRINK AND BE MERRY

TOP TIPS FOR A TRULY WONDERFUL CHRISTMAS

summersdale

EAT, DRINK AND BE MERRY

Copyright © Summersdale Publishers Ltd, 2012

Text written by Lucy York.

All rights reserved.

No part of this book may be reproduced by any means, nor transmitted, nor translated into a machine language, without the written permission of the publishers.

Condition of Sale
This book is sold subject to the condition that it shall not, by way of trade or otherwise, be lent, re-sold, hired out or otherwise circulated in any form of binding or cover other than that in which it is published and without a similar condition including this condition being imposed on the subsequent publisher.

Summersdale Publishers Ltd
46 West Street
Chichester
West Sussex
PO19 1RP
UK

www.summersdale.com

Typeset by Raspberry Creative Type

Printed and bound in the UK by CPI Group (UK) Ltd, Croydon, CR0 4YY

ISBN: 978-1-84953-366-9

Substantial discounts on bulk quantities of Summersdale books are available to corporations, professional associations and other organisations. For details contact Nicky Douglas by telephone: +44 (0) 1243 756902, fax: +44 (0) 1243 786300 or email: nicky@summersdale.com.

CONTENTS

INTRODUCTION

"Christmas waves a magic wand over the world, and behold, everything is softer and more beautiful."

NORMAN VINCENT PEALE

The secret to a successful Christmas has not to how much money you spend, but in how you spend your time making it meaningful and special in your own personal way. The enjoyment of Christmas comes from spending time with loved ones, observing the long-held traditions of Christmas past and making new rituals to carry forward into Christmas future.

With forward planning the preparations can each be an aspect to enjoy. Whether that be enjoying time to admire the lights and atmosphere

INTRODUCTION

" *Christmas waves a magic wand over this world, and behold, everything is softer and more beautiful.* **"**

NORMAN VINCENT PEALE

The secret to a successful Christmas lies not in how much money you spend, but in how you spend your time making it meaningful and special in your own individual way. The true magic of Christmas comes from spending time with loved ones, observing the long-held traditions of Christmas past and making new rituals to carry forward into Christmas future.

With forward planning the preparations can each be an aspect to enjoy – whether that be taking time to admire the lights and atmosphere while Christmas shopping or putting on some Christmas tunes and having a festive baking session.

This book is filled with tips and information to help you keep your cool this Yule and create a festive celebration that will put Santa's elves to shame, including home-made and unusual gift ideas, tried and tested recipes, projects to make and do with the kids, as well as pointers for how to keep the family peace and how to celebrate a greener Christmas.

FESTIVE PLANNING AND PREPARATIONS

> **"** *It is Christmas in the heart that puts Christmas in the air.* **"**

W. T. ELLIS

The key to a stress-free Christmas is preparation. With a bit of forward thinking you can enjoy each aspect of the festive build-up, rather than rushing to do everything last minute. So get your sparkly party-planning hat on and use this chapter to make your own checklist of things to do in the countdown to the big day.

THE BEGINNING OF NOVEMBER

Work out a Christmas budget. It's so easy to get caught up in the festive spirit and end up overspending. As well as gifts, remember to factor in postage, food shopping, decorations, party outfits, nights out and events, and any charitable donations you plan to make.

Tickets to the local pantomime or a theatre trip to see a musical or ballet need to be booked well in advance to secure the best seats and prices – the London theatres take bookings several months ahead, and you can sign up to your local venue's newsletter for details of their upcoming events.

It's never too early to start thinking about Christmas shopping. Start by compiling a list of people you need to buy presents for and jotting down ideas in early November. Underline any presents that will need to be posted as you will have to buy those earlier to ensure enough time for delivery (particularly if they are going abroad).

Post presents early to ensure they arrive in good time. The Royal Mail publishes last posting dates for letters and parcels to UK and foreign destinations on their website every year in the run-up to the holiday season: www.royalmail.com. Surface mail is cheaper than airmail for posting items abroad but remember that it takes quite a bit longer.

Bookmark any interesting-looking websites. Gifts can be ordered in plenty of time to beat the last-minute rush.

MID TO LATE NOVEMBER

Write your Christmas card list in mid November so that you have time to check that addresses are all up to date and see which cards need to be sent overseas.

Get an Advent calendar – it's a lovely way to count down the days towards Christmas, especially for children. Chocolate calendars are in the shops by early November, but if you wait until towards the end of the month you can usually buy them at discounted prices. Or why not make your own? (See 'A Child's Christmas'.)

Get your party invites out early before people's diaries fill up. If you're hosting more than one party for separate circles of people (e.g. family and neighbours), consider having them on consecutive nights so that you only have to clean the house once, you can do all the cooking in one go, get one set of flower arrangements/centrepieces, and so on.

If you plan on doing some of your shopping online, check in advance what your preferred online retailers' cut-off points are for ordering and delivery to avoid the disappointment of a late delivery. When ordering items to wrap at home rather than for delivery straight to the recipient, do it as far in advance as possible so that you have time to check the items and send them back if they are unsuitable or damaged.

THE BEGINNING OF DECEMBER

Give the house a good clean at the start of December. Tidy away clutter to make room for the decorations and get them down from the loft in preparation. Check for breakages and whether the tree lights are working in case you need any replacements. If you are expecting house guests over the festive season, prepare the spare room(s) and stock up on clean towels and sheets.

At the beginning of December, start adding touches to your home to herald the start of the festive season with a wreath on your front door and a poinsettia plant on a windowsill.

Plan your party season outfits in advance. If you are going to several parties with separate sets of people you can minimise spending by wearing the same outfit more than once with different accessories. Ladies, if you're going to a ball and want to get your hair or nails done, make sure you book an appointment well in advance – December is a busy month for hairdressers and beauty parlours!

Write up your Christmas cards and start posting them in the first week of December. This is especially important if you are posting cards abroad.

A good Christmas pudding needs time to mature for that rich, heady flavour – some people make their pudding a year in advance, but a good four weeks should do the trick. A traditional Christmas cake needs time to mature too – about two weeks is the minimum, though many people give the cake a month or more, 'feeding' it regularly with brandy or sherry applied through skewer-holes to develop its flavour and moistness (see the 'Eat' chapter for more information on festive baking).

Order your Christmas turkey by the start of December. You can buy from all the big supermarket chains, of course, but for quality meat your local butcher might be the best bet, and they can offer personal advice on the size of bird you need.

🎄 CHRISTMAS TRADITION 🎄

The last Sunday before Advent commences is known as 'Stir-up Sunday', because it's traditionally the day when people make their Christmas puddings.

Buy your wrapping paper and gift tags early on so that you can wrap presents as you go to avoid a last-minute intensive wrapping session. It also means that should any nosy parkers locate your present stash, the surprise won't be spoiled. Just remember to label the presents clearly!

Get your food shopping done early. Plan your festive menus and collate everything into one grocery shopping list, then do an online order or hit the supermarket in one go in mid December, leaving just perishables and fresh produce for the last few days before Christmas. If you are placing an online order for your Christmas essentials, be sure to book your desired delivery date well in advance, as all the best ones go quickly! And remember that if your order is due to arrive on Christmas Eve, the shop may have run out of certain items or substituted items you don't want; it may be best to receive your order on 23 December so you have time to run out for replacements if necessary.

Make a festive centrepiece for your table. If you are using fresh components such as holly, do it in the last few days before Christmas so that it is looking at its best for your celebrations. You can find instructions for how to make a centrepiece in seasonal magazines or on the Internet – otherwise you can just use your imagination to create something truly unique!

Some people like to get their Christmas decorations up at the start of December, while others prefer to wait until a few weeks in. Decorating the house is a fun activity to do together, so set a date and get everyone in the home involved – plan to bake some cookies and put on that Christmas playlist to fill the house with festive smells and sounds.

Put your Christmas tree up. Traditionally, trees were put up on Christmas Eve, but nowadays many people put them up much earlier. It will depend in part on what type of tree you go for – with a real tree you will need to consider how long it will stay fresh (and make sure you make an effort to keep it at its best by regular watering), as you don't want to be left with a bare stump and a pile of brown needles when Christmas Day arrives.

If you are going down the traditional Christmas cake route, you can marzipan, ice and decorate the cake any time from a few weeks to a few days before Christmas.

Set some time aside in the weeks before Christmas to do festive activities with the kids – see 'A Child's Christmas' for ideas of things to make and do. If you are planning to make any Christmas presents (see 'Glorious Gifts'), remember to factor in time for that too.

Make some food in advance and freeze it about three to four weeks before Christmas. See the 'Eat' chapter for a list of festive foods that freeze well such as mince pies, vol-au-vents and other pastry-based treats.

THE WEEK BEFORE CHRISTMAS

Collect the turkey from the butcher in the final week of Advent. Or, if it is frozen, don't forget to get it out of the freezer a good 48 hours in advance of cooking to allow it to defrost. Check the cupboard to see if there is plenty of turkey foil.

Assign a photographer for Christmas Day – after all your preparations it would be a shame not to have photo memories of it all. These days, almost everyone is equipped with a camera to record the highlights of the day, so you may be spoilt for choice!

Get out the Christmas biscuits, sweets, nuts and fruits and create a festive display on a sideboard or table in the last week of Advent so that you and any unexpected visitors have something tasty to dip into.

Do your last bits of shopping for fresh produce such as milk, bread and fruit and vegetables in the last few days before Christmas. Make sure you have enough essentials to last you until after Boxing Day so that you don't have to interrupt the festivities with an emergency supermarket outing. (Though sometimes 'making do' can be part of the fun of Christmas – remember, the world won't end if you run out of frozen vol-au-vent cases!)

CHRISTMAS EVE

On Christmas Eve, before the children go to bed, put out a mince pie and a glass of sherry for Father Christmas – and don't forget a carrot for Rudolph! It's also the right time to hang up the Christmas stockings or pillowcases, with your children's help.

Do some preparation for Christmas dinner such as making the stuffing mix and counting out quantities of vegetables.

Set the table with festive napkins, Christmas crackers, glasses and cutlery. Freshen up the centrepiece and add extra holly if needed.

SEASON'S GREETINGS

> *Christmas is the season for kindling*
> *the fire of hospitality in the hall, the*
> *genial flame of charity in the heart.*

WASHINGTON IRVING

There's nothing quite like the sound of a healthy bunch of Christmas cards plopping onto the doormat on a winter's morning. Help keep this charming tradition alive and spread some festive cheer far and wide by sending your own cards this year.

When compiling your Christmas card list, work out which ones will need to be posted and which can be handed out at group events or during visits. That way you can limit postage and ensure that the ones that do need to be posted go off in time.

Buy more cards than there are names on your list in case you've forgotten anyone. If you don't end up using them, they'll keep for next year.

If you have a large number of cards to write, divide them up and a tackle them a batch at a time over the first week or so of December. Save time by printing address labels and printing your return address directly onto the envelope.

Cards to be sent abroad need to be posted much earlier (check www.royalmail.com for last posting dates). Take the opportunity to enclose a letter giving news of the family and what has happened over the year (and do try to personalise it to the recipient if you can).

Making your own Christmas cards is fun and rewarding. You can buy basic card-making packs from craft shops; they also offer an array of stamps, transfers, stickers and glitter, so let your creativity run wild. See 'A Child's Christmas' for some simple but effective home-made card ideas.

🎄 CHRISTMAS TRADITION 🎄

The Royal Mail produces special Christmas stamps every year, alternating religious and secular designs each year – these are a lovely festive addition to your Christmas card envelopes.

Most charities produce their own Christmas cards and all of the proceeds go to a good cause.

Christmas cards come in all shapes, sizes and designs and there are some beautiful ones around, so it would be a shame not to display them in your home for the duration of Yuletide. You can buy custom-made card holders to hang on your wall, or try one of these home-made solutions:

★ String some ribbon or thin tinsel across a room or along a banister or mantelpiece, and attach the cards with miniature clothes pegs.

★ Clothes pegs can also be used to attach cards to blinds and shutters.

★ Attach a long strip of ribbon to the top of a door and staple or peg cards along its length so that they hang down the middle.

★ Gather some good-sized dry twigs and prop them up in a vase. Spray the twigs silver or gold and use ribbons to hang the cards from the 'branches' of the improvised card tree. Tie a bow around the vase for an extra flourish.

To add the personal touch to your cards, create a photographic design featuring an image of you and your loved ones or pets.

Don't throw away your cards once Christmas is done. They can be saved and used for craft projects the following year – kiddies' Christmas collages, card-making, decorating gift boxes, making fun oversized gift tags, to name just a few.

A much greener way to express your festive greetings is through an e-card. You can use family photos and clipart to design your own, or visit one of the many websites that offer templates to personalise. Websites such as moonpig.com and funkypigeon.com allow you to use templates to customise a card with your chosen photo, front-of-card text and personal message inside, which are then posted directly to the recipient.

GLORIOUS GIFTS

"Christmas won't be Christmas without any presents."

LOUISA MAY ALCOTT, *LITTLE WOMEN*

A pile of smartly wrapped presents under the tree or mysterious items sitting tantalisingly in a stocking are undoubtedly part of the magic of Christmas. With the right approach you can take the stress out of gift shopping and ensure there are smiles all round when the wrapping comes off.

Letters to Santa don't just have to be for children. To minimise unwanted or ill-chosen gifts, encourage family members and friends to circulate lists of what they would like, or suggest setting up online wish lists. With the online option, items are automatically removed from the list once someone has bought them, reducing the potential for duplicates.

Online shopping is a real time and stress saver, especially if you find busy shopping centres a challenge. Make sure you check final order dates to ensure gifts arrive in good time – many online retailers offer a variety of delivery options including 24-hour express services for those last-minute orders.

A void the busiest times at the shops – early mornings and weekdays are best for dodging the crowds and for getting the best attention from shop assistants.

A lways have a budget and a list of present ideas for each person and stick to it. There is such an array of things on offer at Christmas time that it's easy to become overwhelmed or overexcited, leading to overspending.

S plit your gift shopping up into manageable chunks rather than doing it all in one go.

Take advantage of in-store shopping events when discounts and extra advantage points are offered, and look out for three-for-two and 'buy one get one free' offers.

If you can brave the crowds, it can be worth hitting the shops on Christmas Eve to grab a few bargains as many chains already begin discounting items in preparation for the sales by that stage.

PERFECT PRESENTS

Hot air ballooning, Formula 1 racing, spa retreats, cupcake-making workshops – you name it, there's a **gift experience** to cover it, and they make an interesting alternative for that family member who has it all. Better still, why not create your own personal, unique gift card for an experience you can enjoy together?

Photographs can be used to create a number of **personalised gifts**, including calendars, mugs, coasters, T-shirts, pillow cases, canvas prints etc, either by ordering online or from your local photo-processing store.

Travel-themed items are ideal for someone planning a big trip away – from luggage tags to maps, outdoor essentials, water sanitiser and foreign currency, all these little things can add up and the thought will be appreciated.

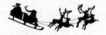

Personalised stationery makes an elegant present for a friend who likes to impress.

Instead of buying your group of friends a present each, why not treat them all to an **evening out** at the cinema or dinner?

A personalised hamper makes a charming gift. You can buy cheap presentation baskets from pound shops and markets. Fill the basket with goodies on a theme of your choice – international foods, pamper cosmetics, gardening equipment and seeds – wrap in coloured cellophane and tie with a bow.

If you're really stuck for what to get someone, you can't go wrong with a **gift card**. They're available for just about any shop, so pick one you know the recipient visits often. High street vouchers, department store gift cards or National Book Tokens allow more flexibility.

Always ask for a **gift receipt** and put it in a small envelope taped discreetly to the present before wrapping – that way, if it's unsuitable, the recipient can exchange it for something they prefer and avoid the awkwardness of having to tell you.

Consider organising a **Secret Santa** amongst friends, colleagues, or even family members. Everyone picks a name at random and buys that person a present, anonymously, within an agreed budget. It means that everyone gets one really good gift, rather than lots of little ones, it saves all involved time and money, and you have the fun of trying to guess who your Secret Santa is.

CHRISTMAS TRADITION

Children traditionally hang up their
Christmas stockings on Christmas
Eve. They must be in bed well before
midnight, because that's when Santa
comes to fill the stockings with presents.

A compilation **CD** or **playlist** of songs you've
enjoyed together that year could make a
romantic Christmas present for your loved one.

Ahome-made **potpourri** or **lavender bag** makes a sweet-scented personal present, and they are really simple to make. Take a length of pretty cotton fabric and use a plate as a guide to cut a circle of about 25–30 cm (10–12 inches) in diameter. Create a hem around the edge using running stitch and leave long tails of thread at each end. Cup the fabric in your hand, add your scented filling of choice, then gather the fabric into a tight ball and pull the threads securely, tying them with a knot. To decorate, tie with ribbon – you can buy cheap 'odd ends' of ribbon in bags from fabric shops.

TASTY TREATS

Sweeten someone up with a batch of one of these easy-to-make, delicious presents and present it to them in a gift box or wrapped in coloured cellophane and tied with ribbon:

★ **Marzipan fruits:** Use white marzipan, food colouring and your imagination to make delightful miniature edible fruit. Knead some colouring into marzipan to create a base colour (yellow for bananas, red and blue for a purple grape colour, and so on) and then mould into the desired fruit shape. Use a fine paintbrush and food colouring to add detail – for example, green colouring for lines along the length of a banana. Cloves can be used to create stalks for apples, and by gently pressing a cheese grater against a marzipan orange you can add a pitted skin effect, or a seed effect on strawberries. A dusting of caster sugar will give marzipan grapes a frosted look. Leave fruits to dry and place in petit-four cases for presentation. Check the marzipan packaging for the use-by date.

★ **Mendiants:** To make these scrummy little fruit-and-nut-encrusted chocolate discs, first melt your preferred chocolate, whether white, milk or dark, in a bowl over a saucepan of simmering water. Spoon onto sheets of baking parchment. Use a round cookie cutter to lightly mark out circular shapes and press the dried fruit and nut pieces into the discs. Leave in a cool place and when the chocolate is almost set, but still a little soft, cut out discs with the cutter and lift off the sheet. Eat within a month.

★ **Peppermint creams:** Mix condensed milk and icing sugar to form a crumbly mixture, and then add a few drops of mint flavouring and green colouring. Knead into a firm, smooth mixture. Dust a surface with icing sugar and roll out mixture to 1 cm (½ inch) thickness. Use a small round cutter to cut into rounds. Leave to them to harden, then dip into melted plain chocolate. Keep refrigerated in an airtight container for up to three weeks.

Another delicious gift idea is to fill a glass storage jar with the dry ingredients needed to make a batch of **cookies** and provide a wooden spoon and recipe card, all tied up with a ribbon.

Always label edible gifts with information about how they should be stored, the date they were made, whether they contain nuts and when they should be eaten by.

Home-made **festive liqueurs** in hand-painted bottles make a tasteful, grown-up present. Fruits like raspberries, blackcurrants and sloes work well with gin and for this you need about three cups of gin, three cups of fruit and one and a half cups of sugar. Citrus fruits complement whisky so use the rind and juice of a lemon, orange and lime together with one cup of sugar and two cups of whisky. Mix your chosen alcohol and fruits together and pour straight into sterilised jars, cover, and store in a dark place for three months to mature. Shake the fruit gin every day for a month, the zesty whisky every day for two weeks, then occasionally after that. After three months strain and funnel into sterilised bottles, fit with sterilised corks and add labels.

MINCEMEAT

A jar of **home-made mincemeat** will look lovely with a handwritten label and a pretty cover made from offcuts of Christmassy material. Have some fun with this basic recipe and create your own personalised combination. As long as you keep the same proportions, you can swap the dried ingredients for anything from cranberries to figs and dates.

Ingredients

- 450 g (1 lb) each of seedless raisins, currants, sultanas, chopped mixed peel, grated cooking apples and soft brown sugar
- 230 g (½ lb) shredded vegetable suet
- 1 tsp each of nutmeg, cinnamon and mixed spice
- the juice and rind of 1 lemon
- 4 tbsp brandy

Preparation method

Mix the seedless raisins, currants, sultanas, chopped mixed peel, grated cooking apples and soft brown sugar with the shredded suet, and then add the nutmeg, cinnamon and mixed spice. Stir in the juice and rind of the lemon, cover and leave for two days. After two days, give it another stir, strain off the excess liquid and mix in up to four tablespoons of brandy according to taste. Put the mixture straight into sterilised jars and cover the top of the ingredients with a waxed paper disc and seal the jar with cellophane secured by an elastic band to keep it airtight. It will keep for up to six months.

Create a **scrapbook** for your best friend and fill it with photos and memorable quotes from your times together.

Make your own **Christmas soap** to give as gifts or to leave out in the guest bathroom. Place glycerine soap in the colour of your choice in a sealed, thick plastic bag and simmer in boiling water for up to five minutes until the glycerine melts. Use festive-shaped rubber ice-cube or jelly moulds and put dried leaves, flowers or slices of citrus fruits at the bottom, then cut away the corner of the plastic bag and pour the soap into the moulds. Create a layered effect using different coloured soaps. Leave to cool completely before turning out of the moulds.

WRAPPING

Rectangular and square presents are the easiest to wrap. Start with a piece of paper large enough to wrap around the present and overlap the two sides by a good 2.5 cm (1 inch) in the middle, leaving enough paper at each open end for folding. Stick the free edge down with tape. Fold up each end of the parcel using envelope folds and stick down firmly.

To wrap a **cylinder**, use the same principal as a rectangular present, but when it comes to folding down the ends, do it in a series of small triangles, folding each one along the circumference down into the middle.

To wrap a **bottle**, start as if you are wrapping a cylinder, but leave extra paper at the neck end. Fold up and stick down the base end as you would with a cylinder. Stand the bottle up and gather the excess paper around the neck with a ribbon bow.

To wrap a **plant**, use coloured card and draw a square big enough for the base of the pot, then draw a triangle along each of the four edges so that it looks like a four-pointed star. The size of the triangles doesn't matter as long as the base is square – aim for them to be long enough to reach the top of the plant. Cut out the shape, place the plant in the centre and fold the triangle sides up to meet in the middle. Punch holes through the tip of each triangle, thread ribbon through and tie in an attractive bow.

S pherical and awkward shapes are best wrapped in thin paper or coloured cellophane that is easier to manipulate. Cut a large piece of gift wrap, place the gift in the middle, gather the paper up and bunch it all together at the top, tying it with a length of pretty ribbon.

A nother option for awkwardly shaped items, or if you are giving a collection of little presents, is to use a **gift box**. You can either buy one or create your own using a shoe box covered with wrapping paper or old Christmas cards. Wrap the items inside in coloured tissue paper and add sticks of cinnamon or potpourri and some Christmas confetti for an extra bit of magic.

PRESENTS FOR CHILDREN

When buying battery-operated toys for children, always include the **batteries**.

Shop early for **popular toys** and **games** as they can sell out fast – for the latest games console or techie present, it's always worth putting in a pre-order.

If you are buying presents for **other people's children**, speak to the child's parents first to find out what they might like, or if there is anything they are not allowed to have. By doing this, you can also avoid duplicating anything the parents might be buying themselves.

DECK THE HALLS

> *"Never worry about the size of your Christmas tree. In the eyes of children, they are all 30 feet tall."*

LARRY WILDE

When the box of decorations comes down from the loft and the lights go on, that's when you know Christmas has really arrived. Give in to your inner elf and take inspiration from this chapter to add a touch of festivity to every corner of your home.

Household decorations start at the front door, with a **wreath** hung from a nail throughout the festive season to welcome visitors into the home. A simple version can be made by intertwining fresh fir branches. Or, you can use a wire coat hanger pulled out into a circle as a base, to which you can attach small bunches of holly, spruce and other evergreen foliage using silver reel wire, or little squares of festive-patterned fabric tied on in a bow shape. Bend down the hanger's hook to form a loop from which to hang the wreath. Finish off with a few wired pine cones and satin ribbons dotted around, and a large bow at the bottom.

Alternatively, you can buy a foam- or twig-base ring from a florist, or make a wire ring, pack it with moss and bind it in place with black reel wire. This approach allows you to press wired items into the base ring, and you are not limited to the traditional festive green. Pine cones and seed pods can be sprayed silver or gold, and dried flowers and grasses come in a range of natural colours: cream sea lavender, purple heather, yellow yarrow, pink rabbit's tail grass, to name but a few.

Drape outdoor **fairy lights** around small potted trees and plants to create a magical pathway to your front door.

Make a **decorative swag** or **garland** by tying sections of spruce along a long piece of wire which can then be draped over the mantelpiece. Add wired pine cones, pomegranates and ribbon for a splash of colour.

An old earthenware jug filled with **silver-green foliage** and **sprigs of red berries,** or a bowl filled with spruce offcuts and pine cones can add a beautiful, natural festive touch to a hallway table or bookshelf.

A bunch of fresh **mistletoe** tied with ribbon can be hung from your doorway – the perfect place to stop for a traditional festive kiss.

Lengths of ivy are ideal for adorning banisters, as they naturally cling to surfaces and can be easily attached by winding them around posts. Give them a good shake to get rid of any creepy crawlies!

Use an assortment of leaves, such as ivy and fern, to decorate **plain pillar candles**. Melt paraffin wax and dip the leaves in it and position them on the candles as desired, then dip the whole candle lightly in the wax, take it out and leave it to set to form a protective layer over the leaves.

Terracotta plant pots can be converted into festive **candle holders** by spraying them gold or silver. Fill to halfway with sand or gravel, wedge the candle in the centre, then fill around the base of the candle with gold-sprayed pine cones or seashells.

Make **old-fashioned pomanders** to decorate guest bedrooms and bring an authentic festive scent into the room. Use a knitting needle to prick rows of holes into an orange, then push a clove into each of the holes. Leave it to dry in a warm place for three to four weeks, such as an airing cupboard or by a radiator. Turn occasionally so the skin texture stays even. Finish off with a ribbon bow.

If you'd like to add a more designed look to your Christmas efforts, try picking a **colour scheme** for each room before you begin to decorate your home. Red and gold against green gives a traditional feel, while silver and gold combined has an air of luxury. Single colours against black can be classy, or go for pastels, pinks and lots of sparkle for a cutesy, girly look.

You can add to the festive look of your home by putting **Christmas-themed books** and **magazines** around the house for people to dip into, and bowls of **festive-scented potpourri** or **candles** to continue the ambience. Small details like sprigs of holly tucked into picture frames and Christmas soap in the bathroom add a celebratory touch that everyone will enjoy.

THE TREE

The **Christmas tree** is the centrepiece of the festive home. If you opt for a real tree, it is worth paying a little extra for a Nordmann non-drop fir which will keep its needles and stay green well into the new year. A Scots Pine also retains needles well and has a good pine fragrance. However, for the best authentic Christmas tree smell and traditional shape, go for a Norway Spruce. A tree with roots still attached will drop fewer needles than one without; alternatively, keeping the cut end of the tree trunk moist will also help keep your tree looking good until the time comes to take it down.

A large circular piece of felt with a radius cut to allow you to wrap it around the base of the tree makes an excellent **tree skirt**.

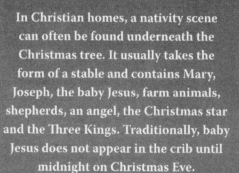

CHRISTMAS TRADITION 🎄

In Christian homes, a nativity scene can often be found underneath the Christmas tree. It usually takes the form of a stable and contains Mary, Joseph, the baby Jesus, farm animals, shepherds, an angel, the Christmas star and the Three Kings. Traditionally, baby Jesus does not appear in the crib until midnight on Christmas Eve.

Home-made **Christmas tree decorations** add a wonderful, homely touch to the room and are a fun activity to bring the family together. Try these simple but effective ideas:

★ Make **felt stars** using green and red felt. Draw around a star-shaped cookie cutter on a piece of card and cut it out to make a stencil. Repeat with a slightly smaller star. Cut out pieces of green and red felt in the two sizes using the stencil. Stitch together with small, even, running stitches using matching thread. Make a hole in one of the star's points and thread ribbon through to hang it from.

★ Use coloured foil paper to make miniature **Chinese lanterns**. Cut a square 11 cm x 11 cm (4.5 inches x 4.5 inches), fold in half to create a rectangle. Draw a line along the length 1.5 cm (just over ½ inch) from the loose edges, then draw lines 1 cm (about ½ inch) apart along the fold up to the first line. Cut along these and open out. Roll into a cylinder with the cuts running vertically and glue the two sides together. Set it upright and gently push down so that the hinged sides poke out. Attach a strip of foil over the top to hang it from.

★ Make shiny **snowflakes** using circles of foil paper. Fold in half and then into equal thirds before cutting shapes into the folded edges. Unfold, flatten and attach to lengths of gold thread to hang.

Create your own festively patterned **tablecloth** using a template – for example a crown, bell, or star – to paint with gold fabric paint onto a white cotton cloth.

Y ou can make a simple **paper chain** using
brightly coloured crêpe paper to adorn
your ceiling or walls. Take two different coloured
sheets and cut 20 cm (7.5 inches) strips off each
roll. Fold the lower strip back over the upper
strip. Repeat until you reach the end of the
strips and then glue those together and trim off
any excess.

An attractive **centrepiece** really finishes off a Christmas table setting. Create your own in a colour scheme that suits – try some of these simple ideas:

★ Make **frosted fruit** by taking assorted real fruit – apples, grapes, clementines – and, using a pastry brush, coating them in egg white before sprinkling with granulated sugar for a frosted effect. Once set, arrange on a cake stand.

★ Spray **pine cones** and **ivy leaves** gold then incorporate them into a display with nuts and clementines.

★ Make a traditional **Christmas wreath** (see p.52) and add four candles.

★ Make your own **place names**. Try taking brown luggage tags, writing on the guest's name in silver pen and tying to the base of their wine glass; or write the guest's name in silver or gold pen on a holly leaf.

EAT

Bob said he didn't believe there ever was such a goose cooked. Its tenderness and flavour, size and cheapness were the themes of universal admiration. Eked out by apple-sauce and mashed potatoes, it was a sufficient dinner for the whole family.

CHARLES DICKENS, *A CHRISTMAS CAROL*

Golden, buttery mince pies; succulent, juicy turkey swimming in gravy; crispy potatoes roasted in goose fat; rich, fruity pudding dripping in brandy butter... this is not just any feast; this is Christmas. With all the trimmings. And here's everything you need to know to make yours a mouth-watering success while also avoiding the bellyaches.

PREPARING IN ADVANCE

With all the edible goodies that need to be prepared in the run-up to Christmas and on the day itself, your kitchen could be in danger of resembling a war zone. The key here is being organised and preparing as much as you can in advance:

★ **Christmas cookie dough** can be made and frozen for up to a month, then defrosted and used up as needed. Cover it in cling film and roll it into a cylinder shape before popping it in the freezer.

★ **Mince pies** can be made and frozen uncooked, then baked from frozen whenever needed. If you make enough, you need never be short of a freshly baked mince pie to offer unexpected guests. Vol-au-vents and other pastry-based treats such as cheese straws can also be made ahead of time and frozen.

★ Home-made **stuffing and soups** to be served as starters such as chestnut and bacon, or broccoli and stilton, can be frozen.

★ A **white chocolate parfait** makes an elegant festive dessert and can be frozen for up to two months and served straight from the freezer.

★ Make the stock for your **turkey gravy** a couple of days in advance and refrigerate. Use turkey giblets, an onion, a carrot, a stick of celery and a leek, all chopped, two bay leaves, six peppercorns and bring to the boil with 1 litre (40 fl oz) of water in a large pan. Simmer for about 45 minutes. Strain and cool before refrigerating.

★ **Cranberry sauce** can be refrigerated for up to a week (see recipe).

★ Prepare the fresh breadcrumbs needed to make the **bread sauce** and stuffing a few days in advance. The stuffing itself can also be made and stored in an airtight container in the fridge for a few days.

★ **Pickled red cabbage** makes a perfect accompaniment to leftover cold turkey. It keeps for up to three months if stored in a sealed jar in a cool, dry cupboard.

If you and your family aren't too keen on Christmas pudding, you could try an alternative festive dessert instead such as a **chocolate roulade** decorated to look like a yule log, or a traditional English trifle, an ice cream bombe or even a Scottish cranachan.

CHRISTMAS DAY DINNER PLANNER

(NB: This is a general guideline designed to help you plan your day – for more detailed cooking instructions, please refer to a specialist cookery book.)

Pulling all the elements of a Christmas dinner together and getting them cooked to perfection and on the table in time to feed the starving hordes is a juggling act that can have even the most seasoned cook in a sweat. You can keep your cool by sitting down in advance with a notepad and pen and making your own Christmas dinner planner. Pin it up somewhere clearly visible in the kitchen and tick off each item as you go, and remember you can always delegate some of the items to ease the pressure (for example, table setting, drinks chilling).

On the following page is a list of tasks, roughly in the order you will need to complete them. Take each task and assign it a time on your planner. Decide when you want to sit down for dinner and work backwards from there. Your timings will all be based around your turkey's cooking time, which is calculated according to weight. So, if you want to eat at 2 p.m., for example, and the cooking time of your turkey is three hours, it will need to go in the oven at 10.30 a.m., allowing 30 minutes' resting time. All the other jobs can be slotted in around this time frame.

THE PLAN

★ Rearrange the oven shelves to fit the turkey and preheat to required temperature.

★ Stuff and prepare the turkey and cover with foil or strips of bacon.

★ While the oven is pre-heating, peel and chop the vegetables ready for cooking and leave in cold water to prevent discolouring. If you have a lot of vegetables to prepare, enlist some help at this stage.

★ Put the turkey in the oven and set the oven timer for the final cooking time according to the weight. Set a separate reminder to baste the turkey every hour.

★ If you are having a Christmas pudding for dessert, begin steaming it two hours before you plan to sit down and eat it.

★ Set the table.

★ Put the drinks in the fridge to chill.

★ Take the cranberry sauce (see recipe) out of fridge to bring it to room temperature and place in a serving bowl.

★ Prepare the potatoes for roasting (for detailed instructions, see 'Handy Hints to Make the Cooking Go Smoothly' below).

★ Half an hour before the turkey is due to come out, turn up the oven slightly, remove the foil or bacon and brown and baste the turkey one last time. Put the roast potatoes in.

★ If you are making bread sauce (see recipe), prepare it now and leave to steep.

★ When the final cooking time is up, take the turkey out, cover it in foil and leave it to rest for 30 minutes before carving. You can also add a towel over the foil to maintain the warmth.

★ While the turkey is resting, put any boiled vegetables, including sprouts, on to cook and make the gravy (see recipe).

★ A quarter of an hour before dinner time, check the roast potatoes – take them out and cover in foil if they are done or leave them for a further ten minutes. Put the plates and serving dishes in the oven to warm.

★ Simmer the bread sauce for five minutes if serving.

★ Drain the boiled vegetables and put them into heated serving dishes. Take out the roasties if they are still in the oven.

★ Enlist help to carry everything through to dining table.

★ Carve the turkey, pull a cracker, put on your silly hat and enjoy!

HANDY HINTS TO MAKE THE COOKING GO SMOOTHLY

★ Brussels sprouts will stay fresher longer if you buy them on the stalk.

★ Don't forget to warm your serving dishes – simply fill them with hot water for a minute or two if there's no room in your oven to warm them there.

★ Have extra oven gloves and tea towels on standby for handling hot dishes.

★ For the perfect crispy roast potatoes, first parboil them for ten minutes, drain and then place back in the saucepan with the lid on and give the pan a shake to roughen up the edges. Heat the oil or goose fat in a baking tray in the oven for a good ten minutes before adding the potatoes. They should take 45–60 minutes to cook.

TOP TIPS FOR THE PERFECT ROAST TURKEY

★ Take the turkey out of the fridge before you go to bed on Christmas Eve and leave it in a cool place such as a larder overnight so that it will start to cook immediately once placed in the preheated oven the following morning.

★ Pack stuffing loosely only into the turkey's neck so that it doesn't prevent heat reaching the centre of the turkey.

★ An onion, fresh herbs or slices of citrus fruit can be placed in the body cavity to add extra flavour.

★ Rub the turkey all over with butter or cover breast and legs with bacon rashers before cooking; season with salt and pepper and then cover it loosely with foil.

★ Baste with cooking juices from time to time during cooking.

★ Remove foil and/or bacon forty minutes before the end of the cooking time and baste again – this allows the skin to brown.

★ Insert a skewer into the thickest part of the thigh to check it is cooked; if the juices are pink, cook for a further 15 minutes or until the juices run clear. The juices will run clear when the bird is cooked.

★ Transfer to a serving platter, cover with foil and allow to rest for 30 minutes before carving.

ESSENTIAL RECIPES

CRANBERRY SAUCE

Cranberry sauce is really simple to make – you can adjust the sugar and orange juice levels of this recipe to suit your taste. Place about 100 g (3.5 oz) of sugar and 100 ml (4 fl oz) of orange juice in a saucepan and bring to the boil. Add about 250 g (9 oz) of fresh cranberries and simmer for ten minutes, or until the berries begin to burst. Allow to cool before serving. Can be refrigerated for up to a week.

BREAD SAUCE

Peel a small onion and stick four cloves into it. Place it in a saucepan with a bay leaf and pour over 300 ml (10 fl oz) of milk. Bring it to the boil, remove from the heat and allow to steep for 15–20 minutes, then remove the bay leaf and onion. Return to the heat and stir in 110 g (4 oz) of breadcrumbs, then simmer for five minutes or until thick and creamy. Stir in a tablespoon of butter, a sprinkling of nutmeg and season before serving warm.

GRAVY

Use your own stock to make a delicious, authentic turkey gravy (see Preparing in Advance). While the turkey is resting, drain off most of the fat from the roasting tin, leaving the meat juices. Place the tin on the hob to heat, add two tablespoons of flour and stir into a smooth paste. Cook for two minutes, or until a rich brown colour. Next, gradually whisk in 600 ml (20 fl oz) of stock and bring to the boil to thicken. Simmer for five minutes and season to taste. You can add two tablespoons of redcurrant jelly at the simmering stage for a richer taste.

CLASSIC MINCE PIES

Makes around 20 pies

Ingredients
- 225 g (8 oz) plain flour, sifted
- a pinch of salt
- 1 tsp sugar
- 75 g (3 oz) hard butter, cubed
- 50 g (2 oz) vegetable fat e.g. Trex
- water

Preparation method
Preheat the oven to 200°C/400°F/Gas 4.

Sift together the flour, pinch of salt and teaspoon of sugar into a bowl. Using your finger tips, rub in the butter and vegetable fat until you have a breadcrumb consistency. Sprinkle on some water and work it into a dough with your hands. Dust a surface with flour and roll out. Cut out large rounds and put into a greased bun tray; add a teaspoon of mincemeat to each one, then make lids using a smaller cutter. Pinch the outer edges of the lid and bottom together, brush lightly with milk and pierce the top with a fork. Bake in the oven for 20 minutes. Use a flat knife to remove the pies from the tray and leave to cool on a wire rack before sprinkling with icing sugar.

🎄 CHRISTMAS TRADITION 🎄

Each family member should give the Christmas pudding mixture a stir in a clockwise direction and make a wish to bring good fortune for the coming year.

TRADITIONAL CHRISTMAS PUDDING

This is a slightly cut down version of the traditional pudding to save time. More traditional recipes require the dried fruit to be soaked in brandy or rum for 24 hours first.

Ingredients

- 225 g (8 oz) melted butter
- 225 g (8 oz) plain flour
- 225 g (8 oz) soft brown sugar
- 275 g (10 oz) currants
- 225 g (8 oz) raisins
- 175 g (6 oz) sultanas
- 50 g (2 oz) mixed peel
- 50 g (2 oz) chopped blanched almonds
- 50 g (2 oz) chopped glacé cherries
- 175 g (6 oz) fresh breadcrumbs
- finely grated rind of 2 small lemons
- 1 tsp ground nutmeg

- 4 tsp black treacle
- 2 large eggs, beaten
- 3 tbsp milk
- 2 tbsp rum

Preparation method

Mix all the ingredients together in a large bowl and then spoon into a 1.2 litre (2 pint) pudding basin and cover with double-layered greased baking parchment. Make a pleat by folding the paper in the middle and then tie with string. Steam in a large saucepan for four to five hours, topping up with boiling water as needed. Alternatively, steam on a low heat for 30 minutes then cook in a pressure cooker for three hours, reducing to room temperature slowly afterwards. Leave to mature until Christmas day, then steam for two hours before serving, or 30 minutes if using a pressure cooker.

SIMPLE CHRISTMAS FRUIT CAKE

Ingredients
- 210 g (7.5 oz) raisins
- 185 g (6.5 oz) sultanas
- 110 g (4 oz) glacé cherries
- 150 ml (5 fl oz) brandy
- 225 g (8 oz) butter
- 200 g (7 oz) caster sugar
- 4 eggs
- grated rind of 1 lemon and 1 orange
- 1 tbsp black treacle
- 225 g (8 oz) plain flour
- ½ tsp salt
- ½ tsp baking powder
- 1 tsp mixed spice
- 25 g (1 oz) each of chopped toasted almonds and hazelnuts

Preparation method

Mix the raisins, sultanas, glacé cherries and brandy together in a bowl and leave to soak overnight.

Preheat the oven to 110°C/225°F/Gas ¼.

Cream together the butter and caster sugar, then gradually beat in the eggs. Stir in the grated rind of the lemon and orange, and the tablespoon of black treacle. In a separate bowl, sift together the flour, salt, baking powder and mixed spice and then fold into the mixture. Next, fold in the brandy-soaked fruits and the chopped toasted almonds and hazelnuts. Pour the mixture into a greased 20 cm (8 inch) cake tin and bake for three hours (cover with foil if it browns too soon). Cool on a wire rack and store in an airtight container for three weeks to mature before icing.

CHRISTMAS COOKIES

Makes around 20 cookies

Ingredients
- 110 g (4 oz) softened butter
- 50 g (2 oz) caster sugar
- 175 g (6 oz) plain flour, sifted
- 50 g (2 oz) ground almonds
- 1 tsp almond essence, if desired

Preparation method
Preheat the oven to 200°C/400°F/Gas 4.

Cream the softened butter and caster sugar together and then stir in the flour and ground almonds to form a dough, adding a teaspoon of almond essence if desired. Roll out on a dusted surface and cut into festive shapes and then place on trays lined with baking parchment. Bake in the oven for about eight minutes until pale brown. Cool on a rack and decorate with festive-themed icing.

And something for the children...

For a fun dessert that children will love, take oranges and slice them in half, then scoop out the flesh. Fill with orange jelly liquid and leave to set in the fridge. Once set, slice the oranges into thick wedges.

SPECIAL DIETARY REQUIREMENTS

Remember to check with any guests you've invited whether they have any special dietary requirements and to factor relevant alternatives into your menu plans. There are lots of tasty, festive-themed dishes you can prepare for vegetarians, for example:

★ **Pumpkin and ricotta stuffed pasta** – works as a starter or a main course.

★ **Winter vegetable filo pie** – the advantage of serving pie is that it goes well with the standard roast dinner trimmings.

★ **Chestnut and mushroom loaf** – a little more elegant than the bog-standard 'nut roast' that vegetarians get served at Christmas.

★ Twice-baked **goat's cheese soufflé** – this one is definitely for cheese lovers.

★ **Butternut squash** stuffed with walnuts, cannellini beans and thyme – a great option for vegans, and you can alter the stuffing ingredients to suit personal tastes.

LOOKING AFTER YOURSELF DURING THE FEASTING SEASON

★ Rather than having a coffee after Christmas dinner, try drinking a cup of peppermint tea to settle the stomach and aid digestion. Either use teabags or a handful of fresh mint leaves.

★ To avoid overeating at parties, have a protein-rich snack first so that you're not too hungry when you arrive. That way the buffet table will seem less tempting.

★ Indulge in the Christmas treats that you really enjoy, but don't feel pressured into overeating just for the sake of it. If you are offered a mince pie or other treat when arriving at someone's house, politely decline and say you might try one later, or have a taste of something offered to appease your host but don't feel obliged to tuck in to a huge portion.

★ If you have bought biscuits and chocolates to offer to guests, put them away after they leave so you are not tempted to snack on them yourself.

★ Drink plenty of water between meals to stay hydrated and to help the body with its job of flushing out those extra toxins from all the rich food.

★ Don't completely ditch your exercise routine over the holiday season. Trips to the gym can be replaced with bracing country walks and bike rides – activities that other family members can join in with.

DRINK

> *There is nothing wrong with sobriety in moderation.*

JOHN CIARDI

Break out the festive fizz, mulled wine and warming hot chocolate – it's time to raise a glass and toast the season with some true Christmas spirit.

The hot drinks and cocktails in this chapter are all best enjoyed fresh. If you want to reduce the quantity you make, remember the simple rule of keeping everything in proportion.

SPICED WARM CIDER

An excellent alternative to mulled wine. Makes around eight servings.

Ingredients
- the juice of 2 large oranges
- pared rind and juice of 2 lemons
- 4 tsp sugar
- 8 cloves
- 1 cinnamon stick
- ½ tsp grated nutmeg
- 150 ml (5 fl oz) brandy
- 2 litres (70 fl oz) dry cider

Preparation method
Pour the juice of the oranges into a saucepan and add the sugar (adjust to suit taste), cloves, cinnamon stick, nutmeg and brandy (or water for a less potent punch). Leave to stand for 15 minutes so the flavours can infuse. Add the rind and juice of the lemons and heat gently

until the sugar dissolves. Pour in the dry cider
and heat until hot but not boiling, then serve.

TRADITIONAL MULLED WINE

Easy to make and a perfect welcome drink on
those cold winter nights. Makes around six
servings.

Ingredients
- 1 bottle of full-bodied red wine
- 1 lemon and 1 orange, sliced into rounds
- 110 g (4 oz) sugar
- 8 cloves
- 2 cinnamon sticks
- 150 ml (5 fl oz) brandy

Preparation method
Place all the ingredients in a saucepan and
simmer gently for 10 minutes. Reduce heat and
stir in the brandy. Serve warm.

BUCK'S FIZZ

Sometimes called a **Mimosa**, this is the classic Christmas morning cocktail. Serves one.

Ingredients
- 120ml (4.5 fl oz) fresh orange juice
- 1 tsp grenadine
- 1 bottle of something fizzy such as Italian Prosecco or Spanish cava

Preparation method
Stir together the fresh orange juice and grenadine in a chilled glass, then top up with your chosen fizz and stir again before serving.

SPARKLING CHRISTMAS CRANBERRY PUNCH

A perfect one-for-the-road tipple, and popular with children too. Makes around ten servings.

Ingredients
- 110 g (4 oz) sugar
- juice of 2 oranges
- water
- 100ml (4 fl oz) cranberry juice
- 1 litre (35 fl oz) sparkling water or lemonade
- Fresh mint leaves and cranberries to garnish

Preparation method
Put the sugar, juice of the oranges and 2 tbsps of water into a saucepan and stir over the heat until the sugar dissolves, then bring to boil for three minutes before leaving to cool. Pour the syrup into a chilled punch bowl and mix in the cranberry juice, sparkling water or lemonade, and garnish with fresh mint leaves and cranberries to serve.

At Christmas Dinner, it is traditional
for everyone present to raise a glass
and make a toast before tucking in.
Recurrent themes are to the Queen,
to absent friends, to the chef who has
prepared the meal, and a simple but
hearty 'Merry Christmas to one and all!'

A **gunner** is a warming cocktail without alcohol. Serves one. Fill a highball glass halfway with ginger beer, add about six drops of angostura bitters and twice as much lime cordial. Top up with ginger beer and serve ice cold with a sprig of mint.

EGG NOG

Keep out the cold with this classic Christmas tipple. Makes around eight servings.

Ingredients
- the yolks of 12 large eggs
- 450 g (1 lb) granulated sugar
- 1 litre (45 fl oz) whole milk
- 1 litre (45 fl oz) spiced rum
- 1 tsp vanilla extract
- 1 litre (45 fl oz) whipped double cream
- pinch of freshly ground nutmeg

Preparation method
Beat the yolks of the eggs in a large mixing bowl, then gradually add in the sugar, beating until the mixture thickens. Stir in the milk, rum and vanilla extract, then decant into a large punch bowl and chill for three to four hours. Fold in the cream just before serving and garnish with freshly ground nutmeg.

HOT CHOCOLATE

Rich and warming before bedtime to give you happy, festive dreams. Makes around four servings.

Ingredients
- 175 g (6 oz) good-quality dark chocolate
- pinch of salt
- 60 ml (2 fl oz) water
- 500 ml (18 fl oz) milk
- 1 tbsp caster sugar
- whipped cream
- grated chocolate

Preparation method
In a saucepan melt the chocolate with a pinch of salt and the water over a low heat. When the mixture is smooth and glossy, stir in the milk and caster sugar, bring to the boil and simmer for five minutes. Whisk and pour into cups and then top with whipped cream and grated chocolate. Sip by the fireside.

BEATING THE BOOZE BLUES

★ If you're having guests over at Christmas time, make sure you have a good balance of alcoholic and non-alcoholic drinks, and always serve something to eat alongside to soak up some of the booze.

★ Appoint a 'bartender' to measure out drinks – people tend to pour out larger measures when mixing their own drinks.

★ It's easy to forget when there are so many tasty tipples on offer, but do remember to keep drinking water throughout the day and evening.

★ If you are heading out for a few drinks at the pub, remember to book a taxi in advance to get you safely there and back.

Feeling the effects of one too many mulled wines? This vitamin-filled breakfast drink, or **Hangover Helper,** will help restore your festive cheer. Blend one cored chopped apple, three peeled chopped carrots and a peeled stoned mango to a pulp. Add 175 ml (6 fl oz) chilled fresh orange juice and a handful of hulled strawberries and give it another whizz. Strain through a sieve using a wooden spoon to press the juice out of the pulp. Serve in a highball glass with ice. Serves one.

BE MERRY

"At Christmas play and make good cheer,
for Christmas comes but once a year."

THOMAS TUSSER

Whether it's making a trip to a traditional Christmas fair, playing silly party games together at home or just settling down with a festive-themed film, there are lots of ways to make merry with family and friends over the holiday season.

A trip to a Christmas market, drinking *glühwein* and browsing the wooden chalet-style stalls for gifts is bound to get you all in the festive mood. Some markets tour towns in the UK over the festive period – check with your local tourist office or council. Others are annual fixtures, such as:

★ The Lincoln Christmas Market has been going since 1982, when it was the first German market in the UK, and now has well over 250 stalls.

★ The Manchester Christmas Markets boast over 200 stalls, including an array of European food and drink, hand-made gifts, toys and clothes.

★ Bath hosts a large Christmas Market in the beautiful location of the city's elegant shopping centre.

★ The Victorian Festival of Christmas set in Portsmouth's Historic Dockyard will transport you to a Dickensian bygone era. Take in the magic lantern show, Victorian dancing and a host of characters in authentic Victorian dress, and browse the largest collection of stalls on the South Coast.

★ The Birmingham Frankfurt Christmas Market has been going for a decade and with over 180 stalls it is the largest authentic German market outside of Germany and Austria.

The switching on of the Christmas lights is an annual event in most towns and cities with entertainment put on, so find out when your local one is and make it a family outing.

The American tradition of putting festive lights on rooftops and in gardens has taken hold in the UK, resulting in some magnificent displays. Why not go for a drive as a family to check out the best decorated houses in your neighbourhood?

Get a group of merry singers together, dress up in warm woollens and plan a route through your local neighbourhood, knocking on doors and singing. Pick a few classic carols that everyone knows and hand out song sheets with the words. Take along flasks of hot chocolate and mulled wine to keep you warm and light the way with candles or lanterns. Hopefully you will be rewarded for your efforts with warm mince pies and even some figgy pudding.

*S*lip on ice skates and glide away in a winter wonderland at one of a host of rinks that pop up around London every year, including Broadgate, Canary Wharf, Somerset House, Hampton Court Palace, Kew Gardens and the Natural History Museum. Or, head north and skate under the watchful gaze of a magically lit Edinburgh Castle in the Princes Street gardens, surrounded by Christmas light-studded trees and with a Christmas market on hand to fill up on *glühwein*, crêpes and roast chestnuts when you come wobbling off the ice. Skating rinks are popular annual winter attractions around the country, including spectacular ones at venues such as Warwick Castle and The Eden Project in Cornwall, so check with your local tourist office for your nearest.

A trip to see the pantomime can be enjoyed by all the family, especially the younger members who can join in with songs and conjuring tricks and really let loose with cries of 'It's behind you!' and booing the villain.

I nvite your friends over for a Christmas cookie exchange. Ask everyone to make a batch of their favourite cookies and wrap them individually and include the recipe. At the party, hand the cookies out so that you all have one of each type to try.

W hy not blow away the winter cobwebs with a festive-themed walk? Each year the Ramblers host a Festival of Winter Walks with guided tours for all levels at locations around the country.

Join in with one of the many **winter lantern** parades that take place annually up and down the country. Try the ancient Roman celebration of Saturnalia hosted in Chester, or the Burning of the Clocks in Brighton – sign up for the workshop beforehand to make your own lantern and join in the parade through the winding lanes, accompanied by drumming bands, to the seafront, where all the lanterns are set alight and a firework display follows.

CHRISTMAS TRADITION

It is traditional to go out carolling or wassailing at Christmas. The practice actually dates back to pagan times and the songs sung during Winter Solstice which were later replaced by Christian hymns. The word 'carol' means 'dance' or 'a song of praise and joy'.

For some nostalgic Christmas merriment, check the National Trust and English Heritage's programme of events at stately homes and museums around the country, from Tudor festivities to Georgian Christmas and even 1940s Blitz celebrations.

PARTY GAMES

Christmas wouldn't be Christmas without the obligatory round of **charades**. Take it in turns to mime the name of a TV show, film, book or song to the rest of the group. Whoever guesses correctly goes next. You could prepare some cards in advance – ask each player to write four cards with the titles of a TV show, film, book and song. Put them in a Santa hat and pick them out at random. The person who guesses correctly keeps the card, and the person with the most cards at the end is the winner.

Divide up into pairs for the **gift wrap race**. Each couple gets a box, some wrapping paper, scissors and tape. The aim is to wrap your present first – using only one hand each. Extra points are awarded for the best dressed package.

In the game of the **mad maharajah**, a player stands in the middle of the room, points to another player and says, 'I, the mad maharajah, do not like the letter B (for example). What will you give me to eat?' The other player must respond with a type of food that does not contain the letter 'B'. Play continues in this way, and with each turn a different letter is announced. The players must not mention foods containing any of them. If they do, the mad maharajah is poisoned and dies a theatrical death (kids especially love this part). The poisoner is out of the game, and another player steps up as maharajah.

The simple but classic game of **Chinese whispers** is suitable for all ages and bound to raise a few giggles. Sit in a circle, or start the game after dinner at the table. One person begins the Chinese whisper by whispering a sentence or phrase into the ear of their neighbour. The whisper goes around until it reaches the last person, who says it out loud – at which point much hilarity ensues at how the message has changed.

For a bit of **minty madness** after your Christmas dinner, hand out an After Eight mint to everyone around the table. Players must place the chocolate mint on their forehead, put their hands behind their back, and try to get the mint into their mouth without using their hands. The first one to successfully eat their mint wins.

D ivide into two teams to play the **orange race**. Each team stands in a line and the team leaders at the front take an orange each and hold it under their chin. They must pass it to the next team member in line, who must also hold it under their chin. No hands or other means of passing the orange are allowed. The team whose orange reaches the final member first, wins.

F or a real giggle, get everyone involved in a wacky game of **Rudolph race**. Divide up into pairs and give each pair some balloons, a pair of old tights and a red lipstick. On the command 'Go!', the race is on to inflate the balloons and push them down each leg of the tights to form a pair of antlers. The first pair to stick their completed antlers on one member's head and paint their nose red with lipstick wins a carrot and a fresh bed of hay for the night.

Did you ever read that famous poem, "'Twas the Night Before Christmas'? This game (called **'Twas the Sausage Before Christmas**) requires a bit of preparation in advance. Get a copy of Clement Clarke Moore's famous festive poem and Tippex out all the nouns and verbs. Go round each guest in turn asking for a noun or verb, filling in the gaps as you go. It is important that the other players aren't aware of what you're doing as the fun of this game lies in the wild randomness of the results. Once all the blanks are completed, nominate a guest to read the new improved poem aloud to the group.

For an entertaining game of **Who am I?** all you need is a pen and some paper. Each player takes a piece of paper and writes the name of a famous person on it, folds it, and places it in a hat. Players take turns at guessing their own identity by reaching into the hat, taking out a paper and, without looking at it, placing it on their forehead and holding it there so the other players can see. They are then allowed to ask the other players questions about the person until they guess who they are.

Stick on some Christmas tunes for a round of festive **musical statues**. One person is nominated as DJ while the others dance. When the music stops, everyone must freeze in position until the music restarts. If a player moves while the music is paused, they're out.

THE OFFICE BASH

Make the most of your work Christmas party by following these golden rules:

★ It's likely to be a long evening, often starting straight after working hours, so pace yourself and make every other drink a soft one.

★ Don't talk shop – it's a chance to all get to know each other better in an informal context. Make the effort to speak to people you don't normally have contact with at the office.

★ Dress appropriately – something smart and with a bit of sparkle, but nothing revealing or too showy.

★ Don't leave too early, as this can come across as rude, but equally plan your exit before people get too carried away and the drinks start to take their toll.

FESTIVE FILMS

There's nothing more festive than cosying up in front of the television with your nearest and dearest and watching a Christmas movie. There are so many to choose from – here are just ten heart-string-tugging, feel-good classics to get you started:

★ *It's a Wonderful Life*

★ *The Snowman*

★ *A Muppet Christmas Carol*

★ *Scrooged*

★ *Home Alone*

★ *The Nightmare Before Christmas*

★ *Miracle on 34th Street*

★ *Elf*

★ *How the Grinch Stole Christmas*

★ *Love Actually*

FESTIVE TRADITIONS FROM AROUND THE WORLD

" As long as we know in our hearts what Christmas ought to be, Christmas is. "

ERIC SEVAREID

Christmas truly is a global festival, with each culture around the world adopting its own traditions and variations. Why not give your own festive celebrations this year an international flavour by incorporating one of these 12 customs?

In the Netherlands Father Christmas, or Sinterklaas, comes early. On the night of 5 December children put out their shoes filled with hay and sugar for his horse, and during the night he sails all the way from Spain to leave them presents of nuts and sweets.

In the early hours of Christmas Day the Portuguese have a feast called *consoada*, in which they set extra places at the table for *alminhas a penar* (the souls of the dead). They also leave crumbs on the hearth for the souls, which derives from the old tradition of entrusting seeds to the dead in order to ensure a good harvest.

During the festive season in Romania, children visit houses singing carols, reciting poetry and telling stories. The leader of each group carries a *steaua*, a large wooden star on a broomstick covered with shiny paper and decorated with bells and coloured ribbon, with a picture of the Holy Family at the star's centre.

Children from Ecuador traditionally receive noise-making toys in their shoes on Christmas morning and run out into the streets to play with them with their friends.

Instead of a Christmas tree, Brazilians have a crèche or *presepio*, representing the birth of Christ.

CHRISTMAS TRADITION

On Christmas Day at 3 p.m., many homes in the UK tune in to watch the Queen's annual Christmas message on television. The very first royal Christmas message was read out by King George V and broadcast by the BBC on the radio from Sandringham House. Elizabeth II gave the first televised royal message in 1957.

In France the big Christmas feast is enjoyed by families on Christmas Eve at midnight and is known as *Le Réveillon*. It is a dinner of many courses, with regional specialties being served, and usually for dessert there is a *bûche de Noël*, a Christmas log.

Gifts are exchanged on 6 January in Italy, the Epiphany, when the Three Wise Men are said to have reached Bethlehem bearing gifts for baby Jesus. La Befana, an old-lady figure who rides a broomstick, brings gifts for well-behaved Italian children.

In the south of India, people light small clay lamps, similar to those used during the festival of Diwali, and put them on their rooftops.

After the Christmas Eve church service in Ghana, revellers spill out into the streets playing music and dancing in a joyous parade that lasts until the early hours.

In Mexico there is a nine-day celebration known as *Las Pasdas*, during which time people dress as Mary and Joseph and go from house to house asking if Mary may stay the night. First they are told the inn is full, but then the door is opened and the visitors are invited in for a party with food and songs, and there is a *piñata* (a papier mâché animal filled with goodies) for the children.

On 13 December, Saint Lucia's Day in Sweden, the oldest daughter of the house gets up at dawn, dresses in a white robe and wears a ring of candles in her hair. She wakes the rest of the family and serves them coffee, buns and cookies.

On Christmas Eve in Iraq, Christian families gather holding candles and one of the children reads about the birth of Jesus. Afterwards everyone sings and a bonfire of thorn bushes is lit. The tradition goes that if the thorns burn to ashes, it will bring good luck in the coming year. Once the fire goes out, everyone jumps over the ashes three times and makes a wish.

A CHILD'S CHRISTMAS

"Christmas is sights, especially the sights of Christmas reflected in the eyes of a child."

WILLIAM SAROYAN

The excitement and joy of children at Christmas is what makes it truly magical. But it's not all just about stockings and presents. Spend quality time with your children over the festive season doing these fun activities together and make memories to cherish.

Create your own **Advent calendar** together – this is where last year's Christmas cards will come in handy. Take a piece of patterned wrapping paper and use a ruler and pencil to mark 24 doors in different shapes and sizes, positioning them on pretty areas of the paper. Cut out three sides of each door – the fourth side will make the hinge. Cut out pictures from the Christmas cards and choose one to go behind each door. Glue them in place and allow to dry. Dab a tiny spot of glue on each door and close them. Add a number from one to 24 to each door, using numbered stickers or transfers. You can mount the calendar onto a piece of backing card to make it more durable. Attach a loop of ribbon at the top and hang.

Make an annual tradition of writing letters to Santa on the same date each year. Get out the glitter, glue and crayons and encourage children to decorate their letter in whatever way they like. You could try using the fronts of old Christmas cards as postcards to Santa. You can even send Santa a letter via the UK postal system, addressed to Santa's Grotto, Reindeerland, SAN TA1 – but make sure the letter is sent in plenty of time as he has lots of replies to write. See the Royal Mail website at www.royalmail.com for more information.

Children's hand-made **Christmas cards** make adorable gifts for aunties and uncles. Stock up on coloured card, felt, crêpe paper, glue, glitter, cotton wool and try these simple but effective ideas:

★ Cut coloured felt into **festive shapes** and glue on to the front of a card.

★ Using paper fasteners, attach **stars** cut out of different coloured card to the front of a card – the stars can be spun around.

★ Using black card, cut out shapes such as a star, bell or Christmas tree. Glue coloured crêpe paper to the other side of the card to create a **stained-glass** effect.

★ Using PVA glue, paint two circles onto the front of a card to make a **snowman shape**. Glue a large ball of cotton wool for the body and a small one for the head onto the card. Use felt shapes for the eyes, nose, buttons, scarf and arms.

CHRISTMAS TRADITION

Before they go to bed on Christmas Eve, children traditionally put out a treat for Santa and his reindeer – usually a mince pie or cookies, a glass of sherry, and a carrot for Rudolf. They must be fast asleep in bed by midnight, before the jolly old man arrives down the chimney to fill their stockings.

Have a festive **sing-a-long** to your favourite carols or Christmas-themed pop music together, or pick a favourite Christmas hit and create a **dance routine** that the kids can learn off by heart and perform for the grown-ups on Christmas Day.

Create your own **designer wrapping paper** using plain paper, potatoes and squeezy paints. First, make your potato stencils. Cut a potato in half lengthways. Use a cookie cutter to press a festive shape into the potato flesh, then cut about a 1 cm (just under ½ inch) thick disc away around the shape so that it is raised. Squeeze some paint onto a piece of kitchen towel, dip the potato shape in the paint and then press it against the paper, removing it slowly to reveal the printed shape.

Use the Christmas cookie recipe from the 'Eat' chapter to make **cookies** in a variety of festive shapes and have fun decorating them together with spray-on icing, edible glitter, confetti shapes and icing pens.

Using a cleaned-out jam jar you can create a **snowstorm shaker** which makes an impressive gift. First make a snowman figure to sit inside, using modelling clay. Fill the inside of the jar lid with clay and make an indentation for the model snowman to rest in and press him firmly into place. Pour cold sterilised water into the jam jar to about three-quarters full. Sprinkle a tablespoon of silver glitter into the jar. Screw on the lid, then turn the jar upside down and watch the glittery snow swirl around the snowman inside.

Paper chains made from old wrapping paper make lovely, colourful decorations. Cut the paper into strips of uniform length and width and hand them out to the children. Show them how to curl a strip around and glue the ends together so that it makes a circle. Then take another strip, thread it through the centre of the first, and glue together so that the two are linked.

Use coloured foil to make twinkling **tree decorations**. Cut star shapes out of the foil using a cookie cutter, or draw stars onto card and cut them out to use as templates. Turn the foil star over and on the reverse, draw patterns using a ball point pen – they will show through on the other side as raised patterns. Punch a hole through one of the star's points and thread a ribbon through to hang it on the tree.

Christmas crackers are easy and fun to make using toilet paper tubes as a base. Wrap a small gift of your choice and put it into the tube – you can add sweets, paper hats, balloons, whatever you like. Kids might especially enjoy writing out jokes to include and, of course, add a cracker snap so that the ends poke out either side. Cover the tube in crêpe paper/tissue/old wrapping paper and glue the long edges. Trim each end, leaving enough to grab hold of. Tie a ribbon around each end. Decorate using glitter, glue-on shapes and stickers as desired.

Make bedtime special in the run-up to Christmas by **reading festive stories together**. You could try:

★ *'Twas The Night Before Christmas* by Clement Moore

★ *Father Christmas* by Raymond Briggs

★ *The Father Christmas Letters* by J. R. R. Tolkien

★ *The Lion, the Witch and the Wardrobe* by C. S. Lewis

★ *The Polar Express* by Chris Van Allsburg

★ *A Christmas Carol* by Charles Dickens

★ *How the Grinch Stole Christmas!* by Dr Seuss

PEACE AND GOODWILL TO ALL MANKIND

" To cherish peace and goodwill, to be plenteous in mercy, is to have the real spirit of Christmas. "

CALVIN COOLIDGE

Christmas: when the whole family comes together and sugar levels hit the roof. Follow the tips in this chapter to ensure peace and goodwill reigns in your home this Yuletide.

If you are in charge of cooking the Christmas dinner, you can avoid feeling harassed in the kitchen by assigning roles to other members of the family to get them out from under your feet, make them feel involved in the preparations, and take some of the stress off you – jobs such as setting the table, serving drinks to guests, even doing some of the washing up as you go.

Always have a jug of chilled water or sugar-free fruit juice on hand and encourage people to have regular glasses throughout the day. This will help to counteract the side effects of too much sugar and alcohol as well as keep people hydrated.

Although everyone playing a board game together is a lovely idea, sometimes this can cause disagreements, especially if the rules are complicated or unclear. If someone has received a new board game as a gift, it might be best to save it for another day when everyone is a bit calmer. Instead, try one of the simple party games listed in 'Be Merry', which everyone can join in with.

With all the build-up and excitement, present giving is inevitably the intense climax of the day, especially for children. To slow things down and allow everyone time to appreciate the moment, you could try nominating younger family members to hand out a round of presents so that everyone has one each, before they can open one themselves.

After present giving, allow a bit of breathing space for the children to play with their new toys, perhaps supervised in another room, and for the adults to look at their own presents and maybe flick through a book if they've been given one – the quiet time will give everyone a chance to recuperate. Don't berate teenagers if they want to retreat to their rooms and listen to music or play with new video games for a while.

Christmas brings together family members who don't necessarily see eye to eye throughout the rest of the year and there are often high expectations of everyone getting on famously for the holiday. This is a tad unrealistic. If you sense an argument brewing, suggest an activity that will put some distance between the opposing factions – going out for a walk and getting some fresh air will help relieve stress and tension.

If you feel tired and overwhelmed, particularly after the excitement of presents is over and Christmas dinner is weighing heavily on you, go to a quiet room and have a twenty-minute power nap.

A carefully thought-out seating plan that places discordant family members apart from each other could help keep the peace at the Christmas dinner table.

If you are recently bereaved or divorced, reliving old family traditions at Christmas can be a painful reminder of what you have lost. Instead, shake things up and try to make new traditions and memories by doing things differently.

Find a way of remembering someone you have lost at Christmas, whether by lighting a candle for them or going to the cemetery to leave a wreath.

 CHRISTMAS TRADITION

In Ireland, Christmas is traditionally a time for honouring the dead, with prayers of remembrance said in church masses. People also take wreaths and holly to decorate the graves of their loved ones.

Don't be pressurised into feeling you have to do something when it's your first Christmas without a loved one – the people who care about you will understand that it is too difficult, and maybe the next year you will feel a little bit stronger and more able to cope with it.

Although easier said than done, divorced parents should aim to co-operate over the festive period for the sake of their children. Share details of what presents you are buying and how you will each be celebrating.

If you are the child of divorced parents and they really don't get on, two separate celebrations is usually the best way forward. Try to organise something special so that each parent feels loved and cherished, and perhaps spend Christmas Day with one and Boxing Day with the other and alternate from year to year.

If you do see both divorced parents on Christmas Day, try to plan it to avoid having to eat two Christmas dinners – perhaps have Christmas breakfast and presents in the morning with one and dinner with the other.

Remember that you can't please everyone – don't spend your Christmas feeling guilty.

I'M DREAMING OF A GREEN CHRISTMAS

"Gifts of time and love are surely the basic ingredients of a truly merry Christmas."

PEG BRACKEN

Christmas is a season for taking time to appreciate what we have – and that includes our wonderful planet. Follow these tips to make sure your Christmas carbon footprint stays smaller than Santa's sooty ones.

R ecycle items you have around the house to make beautiful home-made gifts. Use paint to transform wooden photo frames (unused tester pots from the last time you redecorated come in useful here), or use ceramic paints to hand-paint patterns onto plain white china. See 'Glorious Gifts' for more ideas.

B uy locally made gifts. Many items on sale at Christmas, particularly toys, are made cheaply abroad in places like Asia and their transportation contributes significantly to greenhouse emissions and global warming. By shopping at craft fairs and artisan shops you can support your local economy too.

You can find lots of great gifts made from recycled sources these days, so support these businesses to help reduce the waste stream and promote the concept of recycling.

Avoid buying battery-powered gifts and toys. About 40 per cent of all battery sales are made during the holiday season, and discarded batteries are an environmental hazard. Even rechargeable batteries eventually have to be thrown away. If you do buy battery-operated items, make sure any used batteries are disposed of appropriately rather than just throwing them in the bin – most supermarkets and recycling centres have a battery drop-off.

Don't throw away unwanted gifts; re-gift them to someone else the following year or donate them to your local charity shop.

Decorate a tree outside your home with food for the local bird population – making a fatty bird cake is a fun activity to do with the children, and they can enjoy spotting which birds come to visit throughout the festive season. To make the bird cake; pour melted fat (suet or lard) onto a mix of seeds, nuts, oatmeal and dried fruit. You need about double the amount of dried ingredients to fat. Allow the mixture to set in a container such as a margarine tub or yogurt pot – this makes an ideal feeder for birds to perch on.

🎄 CHRISTMAS TRADITION 🎄

Instigate a new tradition of offsetting your real Christmas tree by planting a new tree each year. It could become an annual family outing to a local woodland project.

Choose festive lights with LED (light-emitting diode) bulbs, which use up to 95 per cent less energy than larger, traditional holiday bulbs and also last much longer. Solar LED lights are also now available.

To save energy, turn off Christmas tree lights and outdoor lights when you go to bed or leave the house – it's also safer if you do this.

Although an artificial tree is reusable from year to year, eventually when it is worn out it will have to be thrown away and will end up in a landfill. Because of their plastic content, these trees are not biodegradable. Do your bit for the environment by buying a real tree from a sustainable, local source and then take the tree to the local wood chipper and keep the chips to use as mulch for the garden. Some Christmas trees can be bought in a pot and then planted on into your garden.

You should never burn a real Christmas tree in your fireplace because it can cause the build-up of creosote, a highly flammable compound.

Instead of buying gifts, give an 'experience', such as cinema tickets, club memberships, gift tokens; or sponsor an animal or pledge to protect a plot of rainforest.

Save last year's calendar and use the images to make your own Christmas cards or as wrapping paper for gifts.

Wrapping paper accounts for huge amounts of trees felled and wastage over the Christmas period, so buy recycled paper and avoid shiny foil paper as this can't be recycled. Try to reuse wrapping paper from the previous year, or other alternatives such as pages from comics, old maps and posters, fabric, reusable gift bags, and minimise tape usage be tying with ribbons.

Remember to recycle or reuse any packaging material such as cardboard and bubble wrap that gifts ordered online arrive in.

Rather than burning paraffin candles, which are made from petroleum residue and are bad for your health and the environment, choose eco-friendly candles made from soy, beeswax or natural vegetable-based wax, which biodegrade and are smoke-free.

If you defrost your freezer before Christmas, it will work more efficiently and you will have more space to store leftover food rather than throwing it away.

Buy large bottles of drinks instead of multi-packs of small ones to save on packaging.

The components that make up a traditional dinner travel from far and wide to reach us, eating up lots of non-renewable fuel along the way. Buy locally produced, organic turkey and vegetables to help reduce this impact on the environment, and carry it all home in reusable fabric bags.

Avoid using paper or plastic plates and cups if you are entertaining.

Turning down the thermostat by just 1°C will save on energy, carbon emissions and money, and it's a great excuse to don your favourite festive-themed jumper.

See 'Deck the Halls' for ideas on how to decorate your home using natural materials such as holly, spruce and ivy, rather than buying artificial Christmas decorations that won't biodegrade when they inevitably fall apart and end up in the landfill.

Buy Christmas cards made from recycled materials, or make your own at home. Be sure to take your cards to recycling once Christmas is over, or keep them to reuse next year as over-sized gift tags or for children's activities.

BOXING DAY
AND BEYOND

"Which Christmas is the most vivid to me? It's always the next Christmas."

JOANNE WOODWARD

Christmas Day might be over, but the turkey isn't finished yet and the holiday continues until the Epiphany on 6 January – so there's still plenty more festive fun to be had. The ideas in this chapter will help you celebrate the twelve days of Christmas in style, and see you into a New Year full of good things to come.

Plan ahead to go for a bracing walk on Boxing Day to blow the cobwebs away. Make sure you know your route, so you don't get stuck out in the cold, and pack a thermos flask and some turkey sandwiches for a winter picnic.

You all enjoyed your Christmas dinner, but come Boxing Day there's still a mound of turkey to get through and there are only so many sandwiches or cold meat and pickle you can stomach. Get creative and put the old bird to good use by incorporating it into an array of dishes – think turkey and chestnut soup, pasta with turkey and pesto, turkey strips stir-fried with crunchy fresh veg, turkey curry, turkey pie, or turkey Waldorf salad.

Simple turkey soup: To make this satisfying soup, strip the carcass of meat then break it up and place in a large saucepan with a finely chopped onion, carrot, some celery and seasoning. Add about 1.7 litres (60 fl oz) of water and bring to the boil, then cover and simmer for around three hours, topping up the water if necessary. Remove the carcass and vegetables and strain the stock into a large bowl, then add the sliced up turkey meat. Fry two large diced potatoes in some oil in the large pan with a finely chopped onion, carrot and celery for five minutes. Pour in the stock and meat, bring to the boil and simmer for 20 minutes. Season before serving.

Boxing Day is the perfect moment to pull out that board game or puzzle that you got for Christmas and all gather round as a family to join in.

Make sure you have some stand-by presents – bottles of wine, chocolates – on hand to give to any unexpected visitors who come calling on Boxing Day.

If you're visiting extended family or friends on Boxing Day, why not offer to bring a course for the meal or some drinks to take the pressure off them?

Always check the travel news before travelling on Boxing Day in case of traffic jams and any problems caused by the weather.

❄ CHRISTMAS TRADITION ❄

Boxing Day is so called because traditionally it was the day when alms boxes kept in churches for collections throughout Advent were opened and the contents distributed to the poor. Later it also became the day when tradesmen, such as milkmen and butchers, would call on their customers to collect a Christmas tip or 'box', though this has mostly now stopped.

The Boxing Day sales are a great time to stock up on discounted wrapping paper, cards and ribbons, ready for next year!

Don't forget to write your thank you letters or cards in the days following Christmas while it is still fresh in your memory who gave you which present. Cut the front cover off old Christmas cards to turn them into postcards.

Going out to celebrate New Year's Eve is expensive and busy. Sometimes it's more enjoyable to take it easy and celebrate at home. To make your evening a success:

★ Get invitations out early – people usually have a few to choose from.

★ Make a playlist of number one hits and popular songs from the year.

★ Invest in party poppers, silly string and some champagne or cava to hand out at midnight.

★ A fancy dress box filled with silly hats and accessories will add to the party atmosphere.

★ If you are serving alcohol, make sure you serve food too.

At the Epiphany in France, *galettes des rois* are served. These frangipane tarts contain a lucky charm – whoever gets it in their slice is crowned king or queen for the day. You can find these in many French delicatessens in the UK these days and it makes a nice little treat to finish off the festive season.

Although these days many people take them down earlier, traditionally Christmas decorations stayed up until 6 January. Be sure to take them down before midday to avoid bad luck!

HAPPY CHRISTMAS!

If you're interested in finding out more about our gift books, follow us on Twitter: @Summersdale

www.summersdale.com